D1524497

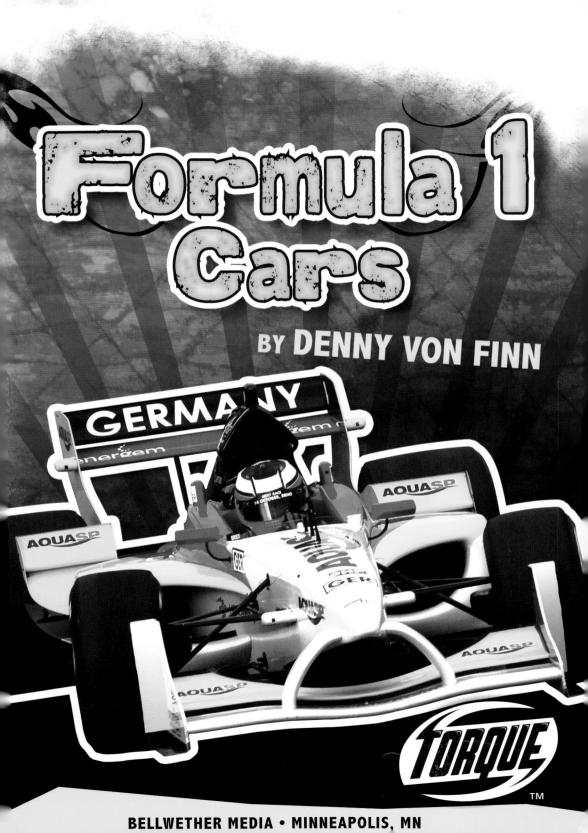

Formula 1
Cars

BY DENNY VON FINN

BELLWETHER MEDIA • MINNEAPOLIS, MN

TORQUE™

Are you ready to take it to the extreme? Torque books thrust you into the action-packed world of sports, vehicles, and adventure. These books may include dirt, smoke, fire, and dangerous stunts.

WARNING: READ AT YOUR OWN RISK.

This edition first published in 2010 by Bellwether Media, Inc.

Library of Congress Cataloging-in-Publication Data
Von Finn, Denny.
  Formula 1 cars / by Denny Von Finn.
    p. cm. — (Torque. Cool rides)
  Includes bibliographical references and index.
  Summary: "Amazing photography accompanies engaging information about Formula 1 cars. The combination of high-interest subject matter and light text is intended for students in grades 3 through 7"—Provided by publisher.
  ISBN 978-1-60014-195-9 (hardcover : alk. paper)
 1. Formula One automobiles—Juvenile literature. 2. Formula One automobiles—Pictorial works—Juvenile literature. I. Title. II. Title: Formula One cars.
 TL236.V65 2010
 629.228—dc22

                              2009008482

Contents

What Is a Formula 1 Car?

A Formula 1 car is the most advanced race car in the world. It is an **open-wheel** race car. It has a **chassis** made of lightweight **carbon fiber**. Modern **aerodynamics** help drivers take tight corners at high speeds. A Formula 1 car can reach speeds over 200 miles (322 kilometers) per hour.

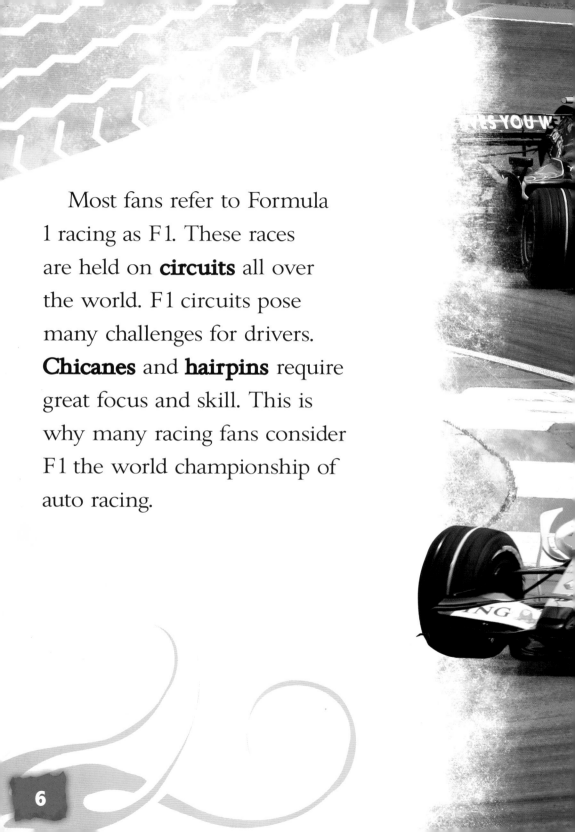

Most fans refer to Formula 1 racing as F1. These races are held on **circuits** all over the world. F1 circuits pose many challenges for drivers. **Chicanes** and **hairpins** require great focus and skill. This is why many racing fans consider F1 the world championship of auto racing.

Formula 1 Car History

The first Formula 1 race was held in Italy in 1946. The word "Formula" means a set of rules. F1 race teams must follow these rules when building their cars. The first F1 rules were created by teams before World War II. These teams had competed in **Grand Prix** racing. F1 races are still called Grands Prix today.

The first F1 cars had engines in front of the drivers. It took a lot of courage to drive these early **open-cockpit** cars. Juan Manuel Fangio was the first great F1 driver. Fangio won five championships racing F1 cars. His cars were built by the Italian carmaker Alfa Romeo.

Formula 1 Car Parts

F1 cars use V8 engines today. These engines have eight gasoline-burning **cylinders**. The cylinders are arranged in the shape of a "V." They are built by Ferrari, BMW, Mercedes-Benz, Renault, Honda, and Toyota. They can create almost 800 **horsepower**. That's more than four times as much power as most car engines.

Fast FaCt

F 1 drivers use thumb paddles located on the steering wheel to shift gears.

Ferrari

wings

Wings keep an F1 car going fast through turns and straight sections of a track. Air passes over the wings to create **downforce**. This force pushes the car to the track surface. F1 cars weigh just 1,334 pounds (605 kilograms). Their powerful engines would make them difficult to keep on the track without wings!

Tires are also very important to an F1 car's performance. Cars began using wide, slick tires in 2009. Slick tires give the cars a better grip on the paved track.

Fast FaCt

From 1998 through 2008, teams were required to use tires with four grooves in them.

Formula 1 Cars in Action

F1 races take place over an entire weekend. Drivers practice on Friday. **Qualifying** races are held on Saturday. Drivers complete laps of the circuit to determine the order they will start in Sunday's race. Drivers with the fastest times start at the front of the **grid** on Sunday.

Most races are around 190 miles (305 kilometers) long. A race can last only two hours. The lead driver wins if the race is not done in two hours.

Drivers are awarded points for their final position in each race. The driver with the most points at the end of the season is considered the Formula 1 champion.

Fast FaCt

Michael Schumacher is the most successful driver in F1 history. He won seven World Championships from 1994 to 2004.

Glossary

aerodynamics—features on a car that lessen the drag effect of wind to help the car go faster

carbon fiber—a material made from mixing strong fabric with plastic

chassis—the frame of an F1 car

chicane—a series of S-shaped turns designed to slow down race cars

circuits—racetracks

cylinders—hollow chambers inside an engine in which fuel is burned to create power

downforce—a physical force that pushes a race car down on the track

Grand Prix—a French term that means "grand prize," and a form of open-wheel racing before World War II

grid—how F1 cars are set up at the start of a race

hairpin—a very sharp turn that sends a car back in the direction from which it came

horsepower—a unit for measuring the power of an engine

open-cockpit—a kind of race car in which the driver is not completely covered by the car's body

open-wheel—a style of race car with wheels outside the body of the car

qualifying—laps driven the day before a race to determine which order the cars will start the race

wings—flat surfaces attached at the nose and rear of an F1 car to create downforce

To Learn More

AT THE LIBRARY

Greve, Tom. *Formula One Racing*. Vero Beach, Fla.: Rourke, 2008.

Morganelli, Adrianna. *Formula One*. New York, N.Y.: Crabtree, 2006.

Orme, David. *Formula One*. Winchester, U.K.: Ransom, 2007.

ON THE WEB

Learning more about Formula 1 cars is as easy as 1, 2, 3.

1. Go to www.factsurfer.com.

2. Enter "Formula 1 cars" into the search box.

3. Click the "Surf" button and you will see a list of related Web sites.

With factsurfer.com, finding more information is just a click away.

Index

The images in this book are reproduced through the courtesy of: Eric Gevaert, front cover; Nestor A. Vasquez, pp. 4-5; Chen Wei Seng, pp. 6-7, 20-21; Shaun Finch / Coyote-Photography.co.uk / Alamy, pp. 8-9; George Stroud / Stringer / Getty Images, p. 10 (top); Keystone / Stringer / Getty Images, pp. 10-11; Getty Images / Handout / Getty Images, p. 13; Rafa Irusta, pp. 14-15, 16-17; Bryn Lennon Staff, p. 18.